# KUDO... ...ck Busters

"Writer's Block ... ly assistance for thos... ...en our creative engin... ...xirs are smart, fun, ar... ...r needs this packet of ... ...e crises hit!" —Da... ...*Butterfly*

"Houston invi... ...cises to approach the l... ...ble bag of tools for th... ...................... .....nagina-tions. I would recommend this book to any student of dramatic writing. Bravo!"  —Janet Neipris, playwright and director of Graduate Studies, Goldberg Department of Dramatic Writing, Tisch School of the Arts, New York University

"In this lively, liberating, fast read of a book, writer Velina Hasu Houston deconstructs and demythologizes the age-old writer's block excuse and restores a plain truth: 'If we truly want to write, we write; and if we don't, we don't. And won't.' This book is part inspiration and part call to action, but mostly an exhilarating reminder as to why we love to write in the first place. Houston neither teaches nor proscribes, she mentors—lovingly, thoughtfully, and passionately. *Writer's Block Busters* strikes a mentoring pose: cajoling and arousing the creative voice. Houston asks questions and shares insights that open and unleash rather than shape and constrain. This book is a gift to writers of all genres."  —Jamil Khoury, founding artistic director, Silk Road Theatre Project, Chicago

"Playwright Velina Hasu Houston has put together a clever compendium of intuitive writer exercises that may suggest to some the classic nineteenth-century tome by Georges Polti, *36 Dramatic Situations*. Dr. Houston taps a wide array of human condition predicaments, philosophical possibilities, visual/sensory prompts, and a little inventive mischief to motivate the dramatist overcoming writer's block or impossible deadline pressures. Classrooms and workshops will find the book essential and clearly the book is long overdue for all our needs today." —Allan Havis, playwright, professor of Master of Fine Arts in Playwriting and provost of Thurgood Marshall College, University of California at San Diego

"Velina Hasu Houston's *Writer's Block Busters* is a feast not only for writers both blocked and not, but for all people who love creativity. This sweet, seductive read ripples with challenges that are just plain fun to engage in at the same time as they expand the mind and muscle of playwrights and theater patrons alike. Here is a welcome contribution to dramatic writing literature that will prove useful not for playwrights alone, but also for screenwriters, novelists, poets, essayists, and souls of light across all arts." —RICHARD WALTER, CHAIR, MASTER OF FINE ARTS IN SCREENWRITING, UNIVERSITY OF CALIFORNIA AT LOS ANGELES

"Velina Hasu Houston has somehow managed to reinvent the wheel—she's found a way to unblock writers' block! This book of practical and fanciful exercises was developed over the last two decades to help writing students discover how to mine their imaginations for creative treasure. Here are 101 ways, developed by a world-reknowned playwright and professor, to 'teach' the kind of intense, intuitive writing that cannot be taught—101 ways to make room for miracles on the page!"
—CAROL MUSKE-DUKES, POET, NOVELIST, NATIONAL BOOK AWARD FINALIST

"Reading *Writer's Block Busters* reminded me why I am so drawn in general to Velina Hasu Houston's plays. Houston has an uncanny ability to take complicated and sophisticated subject matter and write about it in such a way that a broad spectrum of readers can connect with her ideas. She is a magnificent writer, poet, visionary, and mentor. I can already see how I will use many of the exercises she includes in her new book to help jump-start my own writing as well as that of my students."
—PEGGY SHANNON, THEATRE DIRECTOR, ARTISTIC DIRECTOR OF SACRAMENTO THEATRE COMPANY, PROFESSOR OF DIRECTING AT UNIVERSITY OF CALIFORNIA AT DAVIS

"Velina Hasu Houston's *Writer's Block Busters* is not only useful, but also entertaining and thoughtful. Her detailed, specific, and clear exercises are guaranteed to enable the playwright to create the beginnings of the possibilities of art. Her exercises are suggestive and provocative. 'Just a little prod to trigger the senses and get the proverbial juices flowing,' Houston writes in the preface. As Garcia-Lorca says, the writer is the 'professor of the five senses.' Houston brings to bear her experience as an award-winning and frequently produced playwright to the fore in this indispensable compendium, as well as her twenty years of teaching playwriting." —BRIGHDE MULLINS, DIRECTOR OF THE MASTER OF FINE ARTS WRITING PROGRAM, CALARTS

# Writer's Block Busters

## 101 Exercises to Clear the Deadwood and Make Room for Flights of Fancy

### Velina Hasu Houston

**SMITH AND KRAUS**
Hanover, New Hampshire

A Smith and Kraus Book
Published by Smith and Kraus, Inc.
177 Lyme Road, Hanover, NH 03755
www.SmithandKraus.com

Copyright © 2008 by Velina Avisa Hasu Houston.
All rights reserved. No part of this book may be
reproduced in any form or by any means without the
prior written consent of the author, excepting brief
quotes used in reviews. Inquiries should be directed to
Smith and Kraus Publishers, Inc. (603) 643-6431.

First Edition: June 2008

Manufactured in the United States of America
10 9 8 7 6 5 4 3 2 1

Book production by Julia Gignoux, Freedom Hill Design
Text design by Kate Mueller, Electric Dragon Productions

Library of Congress Control Number: 2008927869
ISBN-10: 1-57525-597-9
ISBN-13: 978-1-57525-597-2

*[The murmurs of love and passion] are like the wordless voice of the river itself, a sound that is half water, half wind, or like the tiny ripples that are caused not by the breeze on the surface but by the undulations of the hidden riverbed far beneath.*

—Erla Zwingle, "Po: River of Pain and Plenty," *National Geographic*, May 2002

# CONTENTS

Introduction: Writer's Block? Rubbish.                                xi

The Principles of Writing Exercise Engagement              1

| Exercise 1  | Mapping the Territory            | 2  |
| Exercise 2  | Landscape of Origins             | 5  |
| Exercise 3  | Vanishing Point                  | 6  |
| Exercise 4  | Desire and Discovery             | 7  |
| Exercise 5  | Sentimental Education            | 8  |
| Exercise 6  | Home Is Where the Heart Is       | 9  |
| Exercise 7  | Homecoming                       | 10 |
| Exercise 8  | Lie Be Told                      | 11 |
| Exercise 9  | Some Enchanted Evening           | 12 |
| Exercise 10 | Ten Things I Hate About You      | 13 |
| Exercise 11 | Saying Good-bye Isn't Easy       | 14 |
| Exercise 12 | There Is Something About You     | 15 |
| Exercise 13 | Oh, What Tangled Webs We Weave   | 16 |
| Exercise 14 | All Aboard                       | 17 |
| Exercise 15 | May/September                    | 18 |
| Exercise 16 | I've Never Told Anyone This Before | 19 |
| Exercise 17 | Someone Is Blocking My Car       | 20 |
| Exercise 18 | Tightrope                        | 21 |
| Exercise 19 | Short End of the Stick           | 22 |
| Exercise 20 | Oh Light Divine                  | 23 |
| Exercise 21 | Original Sin                     | 24 |
| Exercise 22 | Being There                      | 25 |

| | | |
|---|---|---|
| Exercise 23 | Second Nature | 26 |
| Exercise 24 | Magic Carpet | 27 |
| Exercise 25 | Our Town, Our Family | 28 |
| Exercise 26 | "When clouds do blot the heaven . . ." | 29 |
| Exercise 27 | Possession Is Nine-tenths | 30 |
| Exercise 28 | Topsy-turvy | 31 |
| Exercise 29 | It's Not Over Until the Fat Lady Sings | 32 |
| Exercise 30 | Bittersweet | 33 |
| Exercise 31 | Fires from Heaven | 34 |
| Exercise 32 | Motherland | 35 |
| Exercise 33 | Monster Under the Bed | 36 |
| Exercise 34 | Pandora's Box | 37 |
| Exercise 35 | The Test of Time | 38 |
| Exercise 36 | Stormy Weather | 39 |
| Exercise 37 | The Heart of the Matter | 40 |
| Exercise 38 | Fame/Notoriety | 41 |
| Exercise 39 | Sensory Apparatus | 42 |
| Exercise 40 | Something's Rotten in Denmark | 43 |
| Exercise 41 | Take Another Little Piece of My Heart | 44 |
| Exercise 42 | The Things I Do for You | 45 |
| Exercise 43 | Neither a Borrower nor a Lender Be | 46 |
| Exercise 44 | Bon Appetit | 47 |
| Exercise 45 | Something More Than Fantasy? | 48 |
| Exercise 46 | This Town Ain't Big Enough For . . . | 49 |
| Exercise 47 | Getting There | 50 |
| Exercise 48 | Great Expectations | 51 |
| Exercise 49 | Naked Eye | 52 |
| Exercise 50 | The Road Not Taken | 53 |
| Exercise 51 | The Kindness of Strangers | 54 |
| Exercise 52 | My Baby, She Wrote Me a Letter | 55 |

| Exercise 53 | By the Book | 56 |
| Exercise 54 | Could We Get a Little Air? | 57 |
| Exercise 55 | Stepping into the River | 58 |
| Exercise 56 | Betrayal | 59 |
| Exercise 57 | Postpartum | 60 |
| Exercise 58 | Living Without | 61 |
| Exercise 59 | Are You Coming or Not? | 62 |
| Exercise 60 | Sense of Direction | 63 |
| Exercise 61 | The Emperor Has No Clothes | 64 |
| Exercise 62 | Sentimental Reasons | 65 |
| Exercise 63 | There Comes a Time | 66 |
| Exercise 64 | What Are Friends For? | 67 |
| Exercise 65 | Organic Ingredients | 68 |
| Exercise 66 | Did You Hear About What Happened To . . . ? | 69 |
| Exercise 67 | Power Play | 70 |
| Exercise 68 | Reunion | 71 |
| Exercise 69 | The Last Straw | 72 |
| Exercise 70 | Old Enough | 73 |
| Exercise 71 | Been to Any Interesting Movies Lately? | 74 |
| Exercise 72 | Sexual Terrorism | 75 |
| Exercise 73 | Tic, Tic, Tic | 76 |
| Exercise 74 | At First Sight | 77 |
| Exercise 75 | Why Should I? | 78 |
| Exercise 76 | Dreaming Big | 79 |
| Exercise 77 | No Accounting for Taste | 80 |
| Exercise 78 | Make New Friends, But . . . | 81 |
| Exercise 79 | Sooner or Later . . . | 82 |
| Exercise 80 | Make It Work | 83 |
| Exercise 81 | Whenever You're Not Ready | 84 |

| | | |
|---|---|---|
| Exercise 82 | For Reasons of Insanity | 85 |
| Exercise 83 | The Movement of Memory | 86 |
| Exercise 84 | Triple Threat | 87 |
| Exercise 85 | My Country Tis of Thee | 88 |
| Exercise 86 | Pollution | 89 |
| Exercise 87 | Wet Amnesia | 90 |
| Exercise 88 | The Three Parts of Water | 91 |
| Exercise 89 | Delusions of Grandeur | 92 |
| Exercise 90 | The Attraction of Opposites | 93 |
| Exercise 91 | Best Behavior | 94 |
| Exercise 92 | I Never Promised You a Rose Garden | 95 |
| Exercise 93 | Seduction Symphony | 96 |
| Exercise 94 | Animal Instincts | 97 |
| Exercise 95 | A Picture Paints | 98 |
| Exercise 96 | Fancy Meeting You Here | 99 |
| Exercise 97 | Beware of Dog | 100 |
| Exercise 98 | Running on Empty | 101 |
| Exercise 99 | I Don't Understand the Language | 102 |
| Exercise 100 | Mi Casa No Es Su Casa | 103 |
| Exercise 101 | The Hungry Ocean | 104 |

# INTRODUCTION

# Writer's Block? Rubbish.

You have heard the self-diagnosis ad infinitum: playwrights, screenwriters, prose writers, or poets who think they have writer's block. They say that they are stuck, unable to make progress on their projects because they feel that they have encountered literary quicksand. If you are reading this book, you may be one of those writers who has found yourself at that seeming crisis point. But allow me to put you at ease, to move you beyond myth that can distract your muses: There is no such thing as writer's block. Seriously.

Believing that writer's block exists and is keeping you from finishing your play, novel, short story, screenplay, or poem is rubbish. It is true that, at times, we writers feel sluggish—deterred by a brilliant summer day or influenza or that what's-it-thingamajig that we have to do right now. Moreover, we are, of course, very human, perhaps even more so than the person next door, so our senses are highly attuned to all the temptations that Mother Nature and our favorite manufacturers have to offer. And there is nothing wrong with following our senses out into the world to investigate life and living, to explore who we are in those contexts, and to consider those with whom we share the world. In fact, they are the wellspring for our imaginations. It is by living and maximizing each opportunity to discover every dimension of life more dynamically that we nourish and provoke our creativity. We live to create—and, for true artists, we create to thrive. We reflect upon and tunnel into the human predicament to mine the resources needed to enrich our imaginations and fill the empty pages. Humanity is our laboratory. When we leave the laboratory and turn to our journals, napkins, or keyboards to use all the stimuli we have absorbed, to let it flow through us and create something—that is the point of perceived creative sluggishness. That is the point at which some complain of writer's block. The coffers of the imagination are full, but the empty page is too daunting. Or so it is said.

The truth is, however, if we truly want to write, we write; and, if we don't, we don't. And won't. Perhaps the latter reality can be viewed as a kind of blockage, the kind that constipates our creativity and makes it hard to concentrate—and certainly to fill the empty page. But let us not think of these things as impediments so enormous that they stop us cold. Let us think of them more as mere stumbling blocks, speed bumps that might get in the way of our literary investigations and goals, but that surely can be surmounted and conquered with a little of the imagination and wherewithal that made us writers in the first place. The idea of being blocked is too finite. It makes it sound as though we need serious medicine just to get through the day, or deep therapy to bear to hold our pens or position our fingers on our keyboards. We have to transform the notion of being blocked to merely needing a bit of help igniting our imaginations. Sometimes, we need a nudge. Just a little prod to trigger the senses and get the proverbial juices flowing.

## Creative Writing Cannot Be Taught (Do You Believe in Ghosts?)

I have been teaching playwriting, adaptation, and screenwriting for over seventeen years. In 1990, I created and founded the Master of Fine Arts in Playwriting program at the University of Southern California School of Theatre; a program that I transformed into the Master of Fine Arts in Dramatic Writing in 2004. During those years, I also guest-taught in the Master of Fine Arts in Screenwriting program at the University of California at Los Angeles, teaching advanced master classes in screenwriting. Even before my formal university teaching, I often led community workshops in playwriting at sites around the country and in Japan, wherever productions of my plays took me. My professional writing career began in 1982 with an Off-Broadway production and a television writing job. I continue my professional writing career in tandem with my academic position. In these many years, one of the most edifying things I have learned is that creative writing of any kind cannot, in essence, be taught. Either you see ghosts or you don't.

What I mean by that is that individuals either have organic writing ability, voice, vision, powers of observation, and theatricality or they don't. None of those aesthetic gifts can be taught. There is no magic pill, tome, or jackhammer that can inject or pummel those gifts into your mind, soul, or muscle. Of course, a lot of writers today seem to have some kind of magic dusted on the epidermis and get by (commercially) just fine with that, but if you are a genuine literary artist, you know it—and own it—down to the marrow of your bones. Long after all the pop-culture/fast-food theater, film, and television writings are relegated to the last click-on pages of drama/cinematic websites, artists' legacies will continue to resonate—continue to be read, written about, and deconstructed by scholars more than they ever were in the writers' lifetimes. Just consider Euripides, Chikamatsu, Ibsen, Chekhov, or Hansberry.

Now it may seem somewhat peculiar for a writing mentor of twenty-some years to say that creative writing cannot be taught. Rather than being taught—and I'll focus on playwriting for the sake of specificity, but it applies to all genres of creative writing—the art and craft of writing are enriched via mentoring. And, yes, that's a kind of teaching, but not in the vein of teaching, say, the sciences or humanities. "Teaching" playwriting is not like teaching the basic principles of biology or the history of Western civilization (although one might learn a great deal from reading or seeing plays about the principles of biology or about the history of Western civilization).

A mentor can guide the aspiring playwright toward a sincere consciousness of the literature of the field: in the reading of important plays vis-à-vis the nature of the student's aesthetic bent and vision, and in the reading of playwrights whose work may share something of this bent and vision. A mentor also can illuminate the shape of a play, the notions of dramatic structure (traditional and nontraditional), and the notion of taking risks but not going so far that the pile of papers on one's desk no longer remotely resembles a play. A mentor also can guide a student into understanding—and this is germane to shaping—what is important about his or her play: Is it a strong enough protagonist? Is it a challenging enough antagonist? What is the (critical, life-transforming) event of the play? Why is he or she choosing to focus on a certain particular time in the protagonist's life over any other (why now instead of any other time)? Does each scene in the play own conflict, challenges, complications, tensions, and progression, et cetera? Who are the people in the world of the play in terms of origins, desires, history, memories, fears, key experiences? And, above all, why must this play, from the writer's viewpoint, be written? In addition, a mentor can furnish a type of concentration and discipline, for a time.

Writing—to breathe, live, grow, and mature—demands attentiveness, both the investigative meditations of prewriting (those moments when one is working and your loved one interrupts you and says, "Gee, you don't look like you're working") and the magnificent focus of actually writing with pen or keyboard. A mentor can furnish these necessities in the structure of a writer's workshop. A workshop both motivates the student to be prepared with new pages to present and provides a weekly, structured environment in which the focus is entirely on supporting the creation of the play. If the writer is truly meant to be a writer, he or she will absorb these skills and sustain them so that the writer can use them to advance toward mastery of his or her art.

Yes, it is entirely possible that I have forgotten some things as I ruminate upon what can be "taught" with regards to playwriting. Like parenting (I have a son, a daughter, and two stepsons), a large part of writing is based on instincts supported, of course, by whatever natural gifts with which divinity has blessed you. When I mentor my students, the first thing I want to know is why they want to be a playwright. I encourage them to read and to talk about what they read from a writer's point of view. Once they start writing, I want to read and hear what they are writing, both in class and outside class. I want to understand why it is critical to write a particular play. I want to hear their peer considerations of each others' work, too. I want them to learn through service and go out into the community to talk to young people who are interested in writing. I want them to think about the world, to be courageous in what they choose to tackle in their writing, to test the boundaries, to turn over every stone.

Teaching playwriting is never an assembly line. Nothing and no one that comes into my workshop is the least bit the same. There are no similar aesthetic visions, even if they happen to be tackling the same subject. Therefore, my approach to them isn't the same; it can't be. I have to consider their natural, distinct gifts along with what I am genuinely able to provide them with as their mentor and the unique ways that they process that mentoring. One may be a lyrical writer. Another may be a highly conventional writer. Another may be a nontraditionalist who plays with language, form, or both. God bless each and every one of them. For three years, I have the privilege of sharing in their literary journeys, and if I am fortunate, they do not disappear. Those who are in it for the long haul reappear over the years. Some never lose touch. It was and is that way for me with my mentors. Because, at the heart of it, writers are a family in and of themselves—a family of visionaries consumed to the gills with utter lunacy. That is the nature of the beast.

### To Own a Boat Like This Costs an Eye from Your Head

In May 2002, I read the current issue of the *National Geographic* and came upon an article by Erla Zwingle about a riverboat captain and his life on the River Po. That article summed up why I write and the way that I think about the writer's life of the mind. The article described the shifting river bottom that reflected on a sonar screen at which the captain barely glanced. He didn't need to. "This is a river that requires experience," he explained. "First you learn it by eye. If you don't know what you're looking at, all this radar and sonar doesn't mean a thing." He can feel and sense it; he does not need to use technology to come to grips with his life's work.

This spoke to me about the notion of learning to be a playwright and the craft of playwriting. All the mentoring in the world means nothing if the natural instincts aren't flowing in your veins already. Your "eye" guides you, never mind the advent of new technology that allows you to process words faster. None of that technology makes a difference with regard to creative vigor if you don't already have a sense of the terrain of the river, the currents, possible sites for stones, where the snakes are, et cetera. The experience will come as you navigate the river over and over again. With the writing of each new play, you will learn something new. Your perspective and sensory apparatus will become enriched. Suddenly, you understand that being at the computer is not what truly helps you write the play. It is you. It has to be you.

As the article went on, the captain, Attilio Formigoni, talked about the hazards of navigating, about low water and floods and whirlpools and sandbanks, not to mention the expenses of buying and maintaining his boat. Playwriting is indeed an expensive calling. Even as you mature and navigate more skillfully, climate changes can challenge you and the subjectivity from the critical front can be crippling. Add to that the cost of equipment, supplies, research, postage, therapy, and whatever demons one needs as literary accoutrement, and one might ask "Why playwriting?" (Screenwriter Desmond Nakano once said to me, "I don't get it, Velina, how can you sit down and write without a glass of whiskey and a cigar?" All I drink is green tea, preferably shin-cha sent from Japan by my family.) But if you have to question the choice of playwriting or you find yourself complaining too much about how hard it is, you are in the wrong room. Despite the rigors, challenges, and incalculable inherent stresses, the riverboat captain, like playwrights at their craft, keep at it for so long for one reason. As Mr. Formigoni replied without hesitation, "For passion. If you don't have passion . . . quit immediately. Because to own a boat like this costs an eye from your head." If you have read this far, I'd lay odds that you long ago took the eye from your head and bought the boat. Sail on.

## Prodding Your Passion: The Hair of the Dog

The best gift that a mentor can give to an aspiring writer is to help the writer prod his or her imagination and passion; to encourage and nurture. Throughout my history of guiding young playwrights (and some not-so-young who have returned to graduate school for the structured concentration and discipline that workshops can inspire, and who bring the richness of life experience to nourish their visions), I have used writing exercises to prompt their imaginations. I think of writing exercises in many ways: jump-starting a stalled engine, sparking a new point of departure for a character or an idea, clearing out the dead wood to make room for flights of fancy, creating an environment where the writer can take risks and see what new places risk taking can buoy him or her, a cattle prod for the sluggish beast of resistance and slothfulness, a skewer to lift the potato from the well-worn couch of lethargy, a stimulant, story medicine, the hair of the dog.

No matter what your creative writing genre, if you engage fully, invest the whole extent of your imagination and vision in a writing exercise, chances are it will either lead you to something that actually becomes part of the final work or allows you to go where you have not gone before; thus illuminating notions that you can use in your work in another kind of way. Students who resist complete engagement in writing exercises tend to be those who are resistant toward and skeptical about new experiences in general, which are anathema to any artist. As with any other passion, you have to be willing to let go before you can move forward. No one has ever deeply loved without taking a risk, going in on an adventure to a new place where the language cannot be understood. Writing exercises demand taking a risk in order to live and write. And if you don't deeply love writing, there is still time to get off the boat.

Writing exercises are tools, calisthenics for your creativity, that allow you subconsciously and uninhibitedly (again, if you are genuinely engaged and invested) to maneuver your mind's eye in new directions with teeth, with the power and capacity to expand the universe of your vision. And that is why I developed the many exercises that I have over the years. I have never been interested in writing the common "how to" playwriting book, and so I have not. Instead, I focus on what mentoring has to offer. Perhaps the education of the playwright is not meant for the how-to book, but for something less pedagogical. While university teaching demands a certain amount of pedagogy, the education of playwrights in any setting requires going beyond traditional curricular structure to embrace the principles of mentoring. There is something to share and to learn, but more in the vein of encouraging the raw materials organically embedded in those who are meant to navigate the River Po. First one must have a sense of the river then the courage to navigate and learn. First one must have passion that invites risk and discovery.

The exercises in this book were developed over the last two decades as I challenged myself to create mechanisms to help my students dig more deeply into their imaginations with the courage to brazen out whatever might be unearthed. No fear is allowed. No "but what ifs." No starting and stopping to second-guess oneself. You just read the exercise and start writing. You wait until you have the time to challenge yourself, sit down with a cup of tea (or whatever your demon is), open the book, read the exercise once, and start writing. Don't think too much. Write on instinct. Don't consider the shifts in the river bottom. Don't worry about any other possible hazards, rules, or boundaries. Go with instinct and passion. And, if you don't have those within you, then put down your pen and go into brain surgery.

I suggest neurosurgery because of something that happened to me at a dinner party once, and that repeats itself frequently in social situations and in slightly different incarnations. I was introduced to a dignified, intelligent, neurological surgeon. Charmed by my profession (his phrasing), he took me aside and started asking me questions: what do I write, what play of mine would he recognize, had I seen this musical or that one, et cetera. Then he smiled and confided, "You know, I've been thinking about writing a little play. I'm going to try to dash one off over the summer when I have a little time off." I smiled and said, "Isn't that a coincidence because I've been thinking about performing a little brain surgery, too, perhaps over the summer when I have a little time off." Immediately, a silence fell between us as he looked at me wisely and I returned the gaze in kind. Without saying a word, he understood that playwriting was a serious undertaking, just like medicine. It was not as easy as grabbing a drink at a local coffee bar and typing out a tome over one or two Sunday afternoons. There was common ground between medicine and art to consider as well. Art and science both heal humanity in their own particular and peculiar ways. Both can improve the quality of life; both can save lives. We left having a more mutual respect for each others' chosen careers. The words "to own a boat like this costs an eye from your head," reverberated inside me. But, of course, I knew that he was still going to write that play, and that he would probably e-mail me and ask me to read it for him. And if it was about the right kind of man in the right kind of societal niche with the right kind of backing, he might get that play produced faster than you can say "new play development." Needless to say, I wasn't going to perform brain surgery, at least not literally. And, for the record, my muses don't allow me much downtime in the summer, which is the occupational hazard most playwrights face.

I hope that these writer's block busters can help to blast away your inability to make progress on your work of literature. At the heart of it, though, you are the true buster of any writer's block that you may think you have. My daughter's elementary school teacher practiced SSR with her pupils: sit down, shut up, and read. So may I suggest that we sit down, shut up, and read a writing exercise and write? We can do it. We must or we gave that eye from our heads for nothing.

—Velina Hasu Houston, Ph.D.

# The Principles of Writing Exercise Engagement

Whenever you feel stuck creatively, use a writing exercise to deepen your understanding of characters you already know or to explore new characters that may bring you to a richer understanding of certain emotional conditions with which you are grappling in your writing.

Just as a writing exercise is a concise, short entity, your consideration of it should be brief.

Read it once or twice, and then start writing.

Do not attempt to deconstruct it, overanalyze it, or ask too many questions.

Read it and write. Your initial response to what you read should be more organic, spontaneous, and rich with emotion rather than intellectual.

If you intellectualize a writing exercise, you may as well put down this book and read a "how-to-write" a play/poem/book book instead.

But if you're ready to be adventurous, courageous, and spur-of-the-moment, then turn the page and engage.

# EXERCISE 1

# Mapping the Territory

If you do not know your characters—as well as or better than you know yourself—your audience will not be able to invest in them. Use these categories to investigate the nature of your character's world.

Birthplace
Nationality or cultural affinity
Race/ethnicity
Coloring: hair, skin, overall complexion
Hair type
Body type (height, weight, shape)
Level of fitness
Physical or mental challenges, if any
General skills, abilities
Diet/tastes in foods
Manners
Posture
Level of refinement
Gait/carriage
Temperament
Fighting style
Relaxation preferences

Personal hygiene
Relationship with parents, if applicable
Relationship with siblings, if applicable
Relationship with children, if any
Personal relationship: lover/partner/spouse
Nature of friendships
Residence (type, locale)
Musical, vocal, artistic/literary abilities
Class/economic status
Sexuality
Gender
Health status
Political affiliations/beliefs
Artistic/literary/musical tastes
Museum/theater/dance/sports patronage
Career or job
Hobbies
Feelings about flora
Feelings about animals, pets
Travel issues, concerns
Recurring dream(s)
Religious preferences
Beliefs in astrology, mysticism, supernatural
Consumer activity
Toiletries used
Favorite color
Holidays celebrated
Memberships

Dark secrets

White lies

Most sentimental object

Favorite possession

Key childhood memory/memories

What he or she feels is missing from his or her life

**EXERCISE 2**

# Landscape of Origins

Place Character A in his or her home. He or she has just risen from bed. Describe the character's morning routine up until the time he or she first encounters another person who wants something from him or her. Then describe Character A's initial reaction and response to this demand. Write.

**EXERCISE 3**

# Vanishing Point

The person, place, or thing that your character wants the most is going away—vanishing, fading, expiring. Your character discovers this information and reacts. Include the presence or essence of that vanishing entity. Write.

**EXERCISE 4**

# Desire and Discovery

Character A has desired something, someone, or someplace for a very long time. Suddenly, he or she encounters that entity for the very first time. Place them at the exact moment of encounter. Write.

**EXERCISE 5**

# Sentimental Education

Place Character A in an unfamiliar environment that is very cold and wet; he or she is not dressed appropriately for the climate. He or she has lost an object of enormous sentimental value and believes that another character—Character B—can help him or her recover it. Character B embodies either the worst fear or strongest desire of Character A. Write.

**EXERCISE 6**

# Home Is Where the Heart Is

Place Character A inside a part of the human body. Place Character B inside the same site. For reasons very specific to his or her character, Character A wants to escape to the outside world. For reasons that are just as specific to his or her character, Character B wants to stay put. Write.

**EXERCISE 7**

# Homecoming

Character A has suffered torture, enslavement, insults, and disrespect in order to return to the side of a loved one. He or she returns home only to find that his or her loved one is gone. Place that sense of rupture and loss in your protagonist. Write.

**EXERCISE 8**

# Lie Be Told

*Truth is beautiful, without doubt; but so are lies.*
—Ralph Waldo Emerson

Two characters have only a half-hour until their lives are at risk. Character A wants to protect and save Character B at all costs. But then Character B reveals that he or she has told a lie about something significant to both of them. Write.

**KEY WORDS:** *loved, betrayed, surreptitious, forgiveness, safeguard*

**EXERCISE 9**

# Some Enchanted Evening

After not having been out together for a long time, Character A and Character B are out on the town celebrating a special event. Character C enters and disrupts the promise of the evening. Write.

**EXERCISE 10**

# Ten Things I Hate About You

Character A is overcome with jealousy and hatred for Character B, who has slept with the object of his or her desire. Character A encounters Character B in a public space. Character B is sincerely inviting and kind to Character A. Write.

**KEY WORDS:** *envy, hate, destruction, stubbornness*

**EXERCISE 11**

# Saying Good-bye Isn't Easy

*What do you mean by this haunting of me?*
—WILLIAM SHAKESPEARE, *OTHELLO*

Your character returns home after a drunken evening and believes the ghost of a former unrequited lover is in his or her house.

**EXERCISE 12**

# There Is Something About You

Character A begins to have romantic and/or sexual feelings for Character B, someone that he or she has given advice to in the past. Character B unexpectedly returns to pay him or her a visit. Write.

**KEY WORDS:** *desire, impulse, risk*

**EXERCISE 13**

# Oh, What Tangled Webs We Weave

Character A desperately desires friendship with Character B, who secretly despises him or her. Character B pretends to welcome Character A into his or her life, but it is like a spider drawing an insect into its web. Write.

**KEY WORDS:** *desperation, reason, consumption*

**EXERCISE 14**

# All Aboard

Character A meets a stranger at a site of public transportation. One of them is about to leave for a train and has something of importance to give to Character A. Write the scene.

**EXERCISE 15**

# May/September

Character A is drawn to a person, place, or thing that is considerably younger than he or she.
An event occurs that makes the difference in age painfully clear. Write the scene.

**EXERCISE 16**

# I've Never Told Anyone This Before

Character A possesses a deep, historic shame about a past incident in his or her life. Character B, whom Character A does not trust, learns about this incident and confronts Character A about it. Write the scene.

**EXERCISE 17**

# Someone Is Blocking My Car

Character A is at the "top of the mountain." What he or she has dreamed about is just about to come true; his or her most significant, troubling problem is about to be solved, if Character A can just get around B—the character, place, or thing that stands in the way. Write.

**EXERCISE 18**

# Tightrope

Character A is attracted to an element—person, place, or thing—that is high risk and possibly mortally dangerous. Yet the attraction cannot be quelled. Then Character A learns that the element may vanish from his or her life. Character A seeks out that element. Write the scene.

**EXERCISE 19**

# Short End of the Stick

Character A is in love with an object about which he or she is deluded. He or she believes that this person, place, or thing is ideal and cannot see certain realities about it/her/him due to the obscuring nature of obsession. Character B, however, is very clear about the shortcomings of this object of desire and decides to inform Character A. Write.

**EXERCISE 20**

# Oh Light Divine

Character A desires someone who is of a highly spiritual nature, one so lofty that the very notion of desire embarrasses Character A. Character A decides action must be taken to express interest without expressing desire. Write.

**EXERCISE 21**

# Original Sin

Character A realizes that he or she possesses free will and that activating this free will can alter one's predestined journey. He or she also comes to believe the following: Every person is born with sin—original sin—but can repent by following a certain faith that explores the meanings underneath spiritual mythology, which enables the individual to unburden him- or herself of original sin. In this struggle of free will versus original sin, Character A feels challenged in the pursuit of his or her desires and asks the question: What is burdening me—god, beast, human, society, or self? That burden enters the scene. Character A reacts. Write.

**EXERCISE 22**

# Being There

Character A is in an outdoor space that is vast and isolated. Character A is there because he or she craves that vastness and isolation. Enter Character B, another person with a tenacious need for that same space for his or her own distinct and immediate reasons. Write.

**EXERCISE 23**

# Second Nature

Consider the dimensions of a season at its most harsh. Infuse these dimensions into your character. Write a monologue about his or her emotions without any direct reference to the emotions. Use only the details of the season's harshness as a means of revealing the character's present reality.

Conversely, consider the dimensions of a season at its most beautiful. Infuse these dimensions into your character. Write a monologue about his or her emotions without any direct reference to them. Use only the details of the season's beauty as a means of revealing character's present reality.

**EXERCISE 24**

# Magic Carpet

Character A finds him- or herself on a small carpet of a specific style and type. It represents everything in the world to him or her. Then Character B arrives in this world. Write.

**EXERCISE 25**

# Our Town, Our Family

Character A feels a strong sense of duty toward his or her community. Character B, a member of A's family, commits a possibly criminal act that impacts Character A's life. This relative believes that family comes before community and asks for your protagonist's help. Write.

**EXERCISE 26**

# "When clouds do blot the heaven . . ."

Over a prolonged period of time, Character A is tortured by Character B and Character C. At the moment the torture ceases, Character C departs for an important reason, and Character A makes a powerful confession to Character B. Write.

**EXERCISE 27**

# Possession Is Nine-tenths

Character B attains or acquires what Character A wants. Character A is crushed, astonished. Character B excels, which involuntarily engages Character A in Character B's success. Focus on the moment of engagement. Write.

**EXERCISE 28**

# Topsy-turvy

What if your antagonist became your protagonist? What if your entire story was now seen through your antagonist's perspective? What is the nature of the antagonist's world? What is important to him or her? What is his or her emotional truth, needs, and desires? With what demons is he or she wrestling? What is good about this character and what is bad? Tell the tale.

**EXERCISE 29**

# It's Not Over Until the Fat Lady Sings

Character A needs something that Character B has; the two are in a significant relationship. Under false pretenses, Character A invites Character B to his or her home. When Character B enters, Character A, surreptitiously dead-bolts the door—a double dead-bolt (figurative? literal?) that requires a key to lock and unlock it, both on the outside and the inside. Character A hides the key and seeks that "something." Just as conflict escalates, Character B attempts to leave and cannot because of the double dead-bolt. (Note: this need not be a literal dead-bolt, but figurative.) Write.

## EXERCISE 30

# Bittersweet

> *... would I ... be ... changeable ... fantastical ... inconstant ... for every passion something and for no passion truly any thing ... would now like him, now loathe him ... now weep for him, then spit at him ...*
> —William Shakespeare, *As You Like It*

Character A becomes excessive with the power that he or she exercises over Character B. This leads to an act of violence—Character A spitting in Character B's face. Write.

**EXERCISE 31**

# Fires from Heaven

Character A recently has changed careers and plans on extricating Character B from his or her life. Character A discovers that an act he or she committed with Character B has some critical consequences that require immediate action. Stoke the notions of discovery and desperation in Character A. Enter Character B. Write.

**EXERCISE 32**

# Motherland

Character A has a deep and detailed ardor for a certain place native to Character A. Character B tries to take it away. Write.

**KEY WORDS:** *allure, desire, greed, impulse, power*

**EXERCISE 33**

# Monster Under the Bed

Mysterious noises, dreams, and water confront Character A as he or she seeks escape from a place where he or she has found him- or herself. A being emerges that your character does not consider to be human for several reasons. But your character needs this being. Write.

**KEY WORDS:** *monsters, humanity, power, magic, perspective*

**EXERCISE 34**

# Pandora's Box

Character A has put him- or herself in a quiet place, a place of simplicity and decency that he or she is committed to maintaining and preserving. Character B, an old friend, arrives with an invisible Pandora's box. Write.

**KEY WORDS:** *expectations, trust, risk, contamination*

**EXERCISE 35**

# The Test of Time

*Time is an illusion.*
—Douglas Adams

Character A finds him- or herself with Character B, a person who he or she has wanted for a long time. Character B has only a short time to spend with Character A, who is also late for an appointment. The clocks suddenly stop, with neither individual claiming knowledge of why or how. And, simultaneously, time flies. Write.

**KEY WORDS:** *desire, discovery, hope, gain, loss*

**EXERCISE 36**

# Stormy Weather

Place Character A in harsh or very unusual weather conditions. He or she is in a hurry to get to a specific, critically necessary destination. Introduce into that environment Character B, a stunning, but perhaps resistible stranger. The stranger relates a provocative sexual story. Write.

**KEY WORDS:** *need, resistance, desire, fear, puzzle*

**EXERCISE 37**

# The Heart of the Matter

*I have the heart of a child. I keep it in a jar on my shelf.*

—ROBERT BLOCH

Character A is in love with Character B, but denies these feelings both to him- or herself as well as to the object of his or her affections. Character B also is in denial of his or her feelings for Character A. Character A secretly has confiscated commonplace personal objects of Character B, of which Character B is aware. Character B confronts Character A about these objects. Write the scene.

**EXERCISE 38**

# Fame/Notoriety

Character A possesses some degree of celebrity and finds him- or herself seduced by a person, place, or thing that is familiar and yet that threatens to return him or her to the anonymity of his or her past. That seduction embraces Character A. Write the scene.

**EXERCISE 39**

# Sensory Apparatus

Let Character B discover what Character A tastes, feels, sounds, smells, and truly looks like. At the moment of discovery, write.

## EXERCISE 40

# Something's Rotten in Denmark

Character A has a deep bond with Character B, but has mixed feelings about this person. After a long estrangement, they reunite. Character B, who is happy to see Character A, carries a stench as deep as the bond between the two. Write.

## EXERCISE 41

# Take Another Little Piece of My Heart

Over a long and arduous time period, Character A has collected or saved something meant to be the foundation of a long-planned investment. But, against his or her better instincts, Character A's emotions for Character B drive Character A to give it all away to Character B. Something tells Character A that he or she is being duped, but the emotions are so strong that he or she cannot control them. Write.

**EXERCISE 42**

# The Things I Do for You

Character A is not what he or she used to be due to rough times, difficult battles, and lack of attention. Lost and on the verge of no return, Character A is saved by Character B, a former friend with whom Character A has had recent conflict. Write.

**EXERCISE 43**

# Neither a Borrower nor a Lender Be

Character A needs money, but doesn't want to borrow it from Character B. Character B has money, but has no interest in lending it to anyone. Due to a new circumstance, Character A is forced to ask Character B for a loan. Write.

**EXERCISE 44**

# Bon Appetit

Character B gives Character A something to eat that tastes awful. Character A is not hungry, particularly given his or her ill-fitting clothing. Nevertheless, Character A feels gracious toward Character B. Write.

**EXERCISE 45**

# Something More Than Fantasy?

> *What art thou that usurp'st this time of night . . .*
> —WILLIAM SHAKESPEARE, *HAMLET*

Character A is in literal or figurative darkness. A white glow slowly appears. A challenging character emerges from this glow and changes Character A's perspective in some organic, immediate way. Write.

**EXERCISE 46**

# This Town Ain't Big Enough For . . .

Character A is or is like an aging cowboy in an aging town, but it is his or her town, and so he or she is bound and determined to love it. Character B arrives bringing news that he or she believes will make Character A need to leave town. The characters have an awkward history. Write.

**KEY WORDS:** *hired, reckless, roping, dirt, nomad, lonesome*

**EXERCISE 47**

# Getting There

> *Love can transpose to form and dignity:*
> *Love looks not with the eyes, but with the mind;*
> *And therefore is wing'd Cupid painted blind . . .*
> —WILLIAM SHAKESPEARE, *A MIDSUMMER NIGHT'S DREAM*

Character A moves to a site of myth and magic to restore his or her spirits and dignity. It is a site that cannot be reached by any means of modern transportation. Character B, the source of the loss of Character A's poise and self-esteem, arrives unexpectedly—although in some way Character A had a premonition of the arrival. Write.

**EXERCISE 48**

# Great Expectations

*Oft expectation fails and most oft there
Where most it promises . . .*
   —WILLIAM SHAKESPEARE, *ALL'S WELL THAT ENDS WELL*

Character A believes that he or she is at home alone. Character A engages in an activity that usually requires being alone. Unexpectedly, Character B enters. Write.

**EXERCISE 49**

# Naked Eye

In the midst of a routine but time-dependent task, Character A becomes very ill. Character B, with whom Character A shares an uneasy and embarrassing past, enters. Write.

**EXERCISE 50**

# The Road Not Taken

Character A finds him- or herself at a crossroads in oppressive weather. One path involves Character B. One path involves Character C. Character A chooses a path and faces challenges involving both Characters B and C. Write.

**EXERCISE 51**

# The Kindness of Strangers

Character B commits an act of kindness for Character A. Character A imprisons, detains, or locks up Character B, making B subject to his or her power. Write.

**KEY WORDS:** *subjugation, rebellion, threat, ineptitude*

**EXERCISE 52**

# My Baby, She Wrote Me a Letter

Character A asks or hires Character B to write a letter for him or her. The letter is to someone whom Character A believes can change his or her life. Because of a past tie with the letter's recipient, Character B is reluctant to write the letter. Write.

**EXERCISE 53**

# By the Book

Character A and Character B share a close bond and also work together. Character A discovers something amiss in his or her work environment. Because of Character B's vested interests in the work environment, he or she must protect its reputation. Character A is equally committed to reveal the problem motivated by what he or she defines as integrity. Write.

**KEY WORDS:** *personal interests, disinfecting one's society, conscience, mutability of public opinion*

**EXERCISE 54**

# Could We Get a Little Air?

Character A believes in truth and freedom. Character A finds out that his or her relationship with Character B is based on a lie. To confront it means ruining the relationship, which Character A believes is the only means to save it. Character B believes that their relationship is rich with integrity and takes the stability of the relationship as a given. There is a distinct lack of oxygen in the room. Write.

**KEY WORDS:** *truth, friend, enemy, inconsistency of principles, breathe, window, what will people think*

**EXERCISE 55**

# Stepping into the River

Character A returns to Character B after a long absence, but there is something fleeting about Character A's presence. Write.

**KEY WORDS:** *repetition, music, water, dissolve*

**EXERCISE 56**

# Betrayal

Important, critical knowledge is shared by Characters A and B. Character B has power over Character A. Character A gives this knowledge to Character C. Character B wants to punish him or her for this perceived indiscretion. Write.

**EXERCISE 57**

# Postpartum

Character A gives birth to something important, but it is a painful process that alters his or her perspective about the future. Character B, whose future is bright, played a part in the birth. Character B arrives in the aftermath. Write.

**EXERCISE 58**

# Living Without

Character A stands to lose something or someone of great value. Character B, a business partner and friend who claims to have Character A's best interests at heart, increases the risk. Write.

**EXERCISE 59**

# Are You Coming or Not?

Character A has thirty minutes to convince Character B to take a journey with him or her. Character B is exhausted and on the verge of collapse. Write.

**EXERCISE 60**

# Sense of Direction

Character A can't read the map that explains the way. Character B detests maps and relies solely on instinct. The two characters need each other. Write.

**EXERCISE 61**

# The Emperor Has No Clothes

Focus on a real-life character with whom you are fascinated and the nature of his or her situation that intrigues you. Take these perceptions and place them in the character in your story. Give the character an incident or event that robs him or her of most, if not all, of these attributes. Write.

**EXERCISE 62**

# Sentimental Reasons

Character A cherishes a sentimental object that dates back to his or her childhood. It continues to create intense feelings in Character A including desire. These feelings come to bear anew when Character B seeks to destroy Character A's sentiments. Character B embodies either the worst fear or strongest desire of Character A. Give Character A the sense of being underdressed in an unfamiliar environment that is very cold and wet. Write.

**EXERCISE 63**

# There Comes a Time

Character A writes a letter to a loved one being left behind and who doesn't want to be left behind. Character A's letter explores the notion that he or she is about to embark upon an important journey and he or she attempts to justify his or her reasons for having to go. The loved one is present and resistant. Write.

**EXERCISE 64**

# What Are Friends For?

Character A likes his or her home just the way it is. Good friends—Characters B and C—show up needing a place to stay, but refuse to explain why. Immediately, they take control of Character A's home. Write.

**EXERCISE 65**

# Organic Ingredients

Take a belief in magic, a knack for capital enterprise despite financial constraints, the need to find a lost loved one, and the need to be touched. Place these ingredients into Character A and locate Character A in a place that he or she has never been before. Bring a stranger into this environment. Write.

# EXERCISE 66

# Did You Hear About What Happened To . . . ?

Character A discovers the "death" of an object of desire (person, place, or thing). Character A is in grief, mourning the loss. This grief makes his or her behaviors extreme: Character A is angry, sullen, and embarrassingly emotional. The person Character A blames for his or her loss enters. Write.

**EXERCISE 67**

# Power Play

Character A feels powerful about a certain aspect of his or her life, and he or she takes pleasure in that power. But then the mental and physical health of Character B forces a sense of overall disempowerment in Character A's life. Write.

**EXERCISE 68**

# Reunion

Character B—who Character A has not seen for a long, long time—suddenly writes Character A. Despite the climate (geographical and emotional), Character A decides to find Character B because of the letter. They agree to meet at the last place they saw each other. They meet. Write.

**EXERCISE 69**

# The Last Straw

Character A discovers that he or she has a capacity for violence. Character B enters and unwittingly challenges the threshold of Character A's violence. Write.

**EXERCISE 70**

# Old Enough

Character A deeply desires something, someone, or some place, but is denied access to this entity because of his or her age. The person that denies access enters Character A's space. Write.

**EXERCISE 71**

# Been to Any Interesting Movies Lately?

Character A has discovered something odd about Character B that makes Character A wary of Character B and their imminent relationship, but Character A cannot bring him- or herself to discuss the discovery directly. Write.

**EXERCISE 72**

# Sexual Terrorism

Character A announces to Character B that there will be a moratorium on sex in their relationship until Character B agrees to address an uncomfortable subject with him or her. But Character B thinks the moratorium is a reason to celebrate, a vacation. Write.

**EXERCISE 73**

# Tic, Tic, Tic

Character A is fond of Character B, but Character B does not yet know it. There is something about Character B—a physically undesirable habit—that Character A wants to tell Character B about, but cannot. Write.

**EXERCISE 74**

# At First Sight

Characters A and B have just met and are extremely attracted to one another, but circumstances due to weather and family relations—not to mention personal integrity—are keeping them from expressing any interest. Nevertheless, they find themselves in close proximity in a public setting. Write what they *can* say, with what they want to say just under the surface. Yet each must be pursuing an action in what they *do* say.

**EXERCISE 75**

# Why Should I?

Characters A and B are stuck in an elevator together. The emergency phone doesn't work and neither of their cell phones can get a signal in the lift. One character does not trust the other. One character is highly aggressive. Write.

**EXERCISE 76**

# Dreaming Big

*Those who dream by day are cognizant of many things which escape those who dream only by night.*
—Edgar Allan Poe

Record the last dream of your protagonist in detail. Take the fiercest emotion from the dream. Put it into another chief character from your play as he or she exists at this very moment. Put the two characters in the same site, a site from which neither can physically escape. Write.

**EXERCISE 77**

# No Accounting for Taste

Character A purchases a gift for Character B that is very expensive. It is a personal gift—one that B would have to wear or that would be seen in public. Character A presents it to Character B. B does not like it—it is too vulgar, peculiar, or nondescript—but cannot reveal his or her distaste for it outwardly. (Perhaps Character C enters and is not afraid to express his or her negative opinions about the gift.) Write.

**EXERCISE 78**

# Make New Friends, But . . .

Character A's best friend, Character B, takes him or her to an idyllic place and makes an announcement of compromising behavior with Character A's partner, lover, or spouse. Write.

**EXERCISE 79**

# Sooner or Later . . .

Character A is living a lie that no one has been able to discover. An event occurs that exposes this lie. Enter Character B, the person responsible for exposing the lie. Write. Focus on the complications that emerge from the lie and the actions they motivate.

**EXERCISE 80**

# Make It Work

Character A's engine breaks down, and Character B forces him or her to look under the hood and try to fix it. Write. Don't be afraid to think figuratively.

**EXERCISE 81**

# Whenever You're Not Ready

Irrationality, earthiness, heightened awareness of death, diabolical nature—place all four of these elements into Character A. Bring into the scene an object of his or her deepest desire. Write.

**EXERCISE 82**

# For Reasons of Insanity

Character A believes that he or she exists in a state of contentment. At least for this very moment, Character A believes that all is well in life, primarily based on the solid love that he or she shares with Character B. But then an incident occurs that leads Character A to discover that Character B is in love with an inanimate and inappropriate object. At the moment of discovery, enter Character B. Write.

**EXERCISE 83**

# The Movement of Memory

Character A has three distinct memories from his or her early life, and A keeps them alive at all cost in his or her current life. These memories have something to do with shape, posture, and gait. Character B discovers that he or she has no memories about his or her past. He or she wants a memory. Write.

**EXERCISE 84**

# Triple Threat

Consider your character's deepest shame, deepest fear, and deepest desire. Introduce a character that embodies all three elements. Write.

**EXERCISE 85**

# My Country Tis of Thee

Character A leaves his or her community for Character B, then is betrayed or abandoned by Character B, causing a major loss. Character A decides to confront Character B. Write.

**EXERCISE 86**

# Pollution

Character A lives in a beautiful, well-maintained place. Character B's home is a mess and Character A refuses to enter, but then he or she must. Character B discovers that Character A's dirt and disorder are inside him or her. Write.

**EXERCISE 87**

# Wet Amnesia

Character A feels alive and vital. Character B arrives and claims that Character A wept for months for his or her return. Character A cannot remember doing so. Write.

**EXERCISE 88**

# The Three Parts of Water

*If I see the sea*
*I think that's where*
*my soul should be . . .*

—Marin Sorescu

Character A cannot get enough water to drink. Character B is sweating and wants to bathe. There is no rain. There is too much food. They cannot leave. Write.

**EXERCISE 89**

# Delusions of Grandeur

Character A believes that Character B's perception of others' awareness of and interest in him or her and his or her work is exaggerated. Character B reports another larger-than-life view of his or her exploits. Character A believes he or she is embroidering the event in the retelling. Incredibly, it is snowing outside and the roads are closed. Write.

**EXERCISE 90**

# The Attraction of Opposites

Character A loathes the opposite sex for a very specific reason. Enter Character B who appears to be a member of the same sex as Character A. Character A does not recognize that this A's former close-friend-with-benefits who now loves his or her "new" opposite sex, but is repelled by A's gender. Write.

**EXERCISE 91**

# Best Behavior

Character A must speak with Character B, a respected individual who has considerable control over Character A's future, about an act committed by Character B that is seen by Character A as a considerable indiscretion. Write.

**EXERCISE 92**

# I Never Promised You a Rose Garden

Character A discovers that Character B, his or her partner, has used Character A as a pawn. But confronting Character B is challenging because of a risk of violence. In fact, it is in Character A's best interest to have Character B continue to believe that Character A adores him or her. Focus on the moment Character A discovers the deception. Write.

**EXERCISE 93**

# Seduction Symphony

Character A plays music in order to reach beyond the grave to Character B. Write.

**EXERCISE 94**

# Animal Instincts

Two characters exist in different time periods so that their lives are never in synch. If either encountered the other's reality, he or she would perceive that reality as surreal—so different are their worlds. A synchronization occurs. Write.

**EXERCISE 95**

# A Picture Paints

Select a painting or photograph you like. Place your character in this painting and use all elements of the painting (light, color, place, characters, mood, theme, time) as well as the senses as points of departure for desire and conflict for your character. Write.

**EXERCISE 96**

# Fancy Meeting You Here

Character A is in a hurry to keep a pressing appointment that can never be rescheduled. He or she falls into a hole. Character B is already in the hole. Write.

**EXERCISE 97**

# Beware of Dog

Character A strikes a deal with Character B, only to have Character B renege on the deal and vanish, causing Character A great shame and hardship. Character B returns. Write, beginning at the exact moment of Character B's return.

## EXERCISE 98

# Running on Empty

Character A has given up everything of significance in his or her life to be with Character B. They are in a place that is new to both of them. Character B is disillusioned by Character A's inability to survive in this new place. Character A feels vengeful. Write.

**EXERCISE 99**

# I Don't Understand the Language

Character A finds him- or herself in a foreign place in which what he or she says is not readily understood. Character B has the power to make Character A comfortable in this place but also makes demands that compromises Character A's financial stability. Write.

**EXERCISE 100**

# Mi Casa No Es Su Casa

Character A owns a certain territory that reflects his or her power and legacy. Character B wants the territory and is ready to obtain it by any means necessary. Write.

**EXERCISE 101**

# The Hungry Ocean

> *When I have seen by Time's fell hand defaced*
> *The rich proud cost of outworn buried age;*
> *When sometime lofty towers I see down-razed*
> *And brass eternal slave to mortal rage;*
> *When I have seen the hungry ocean gain*
> *Advantage on the kingdom of the shore,*
> *And the firm soil in of the watery main,*
> *Increasing store with loss and loss with store . . .*
> —William Shakespeare, Sonnet LXIV

Character A has caused the physical or emotional death of someone who is essential to the peace of mind of Character B. Character A wishes to make amends in a way that makes no sense to Character B. Write.

# About the Author

Since her work first appeared Off-Broadway in the 1980s, Velina Hasu Houston has written over thirty plays, fourteen commissioned. She is Professor of Theatre, Director of Dramatic Writing, Resident Playwright, and Associate Dean of Faculty at the University of Southern California School of Theatre. Houston's plays have appeared internationally at Manhattan Theatre Club, Pasadena Playhouse, Old Globe Theatre, George Street Playhouse, Pittsburgh Public Theatre, Smithsonian Institution, Whole Theatre/Olympia Dukakis, Nippon Hoso Kai, Negro Ensemble, Syracuse Stage, Mixed Blood Theatre, and others.